C

1

Antlers for Alastair

"Father Christmas does not sing with a reggae band," sighed Miss Mopper.

"But Miss!" cried Lennox, "my brother and his band could come and play for me. There are nine of them."

"Lennox. I said NO. I just want you to be Father Christmas without any drums or guitars. Now, what does Father Christmas say first?"

Lennox frowned. Then he said in a very deep voice,

"HO HO children! Here I come.
Leave me egg and chips and a glass of rum!"

"Errr . . . we may think of something better than that," said Miss Mopper. "You see, children, it is our turn to perform the Christmas play this year. And I want it to be THE BEST PLAY EVER!"

Her class cheered and clapped and Miss

Mopper jumped onto the stage and spun round with her arms outstretched.

"I have written our own special play," she cried, her eyes shining. "I spent all weekend thinking about it. We have only two weeks to practise. We will perform the play for the whole school and all the parents and visitors at seven o'clock on Friday the thirteenth of December. I want you to make up your own words if you can. If not, I will help. You can all have a part if you like."

"What? Even Alastair?" sneered a voice from the back of the hall.

"Yes, Darrill," said Miss Mopper crossly. "Of course there is a part for Alastair, a very important part indeed."

Alastair's ears went red with happiness and he hid his face in his jumper.

"What part will Alastair have, Miss?" asked Michael who was sitting next to him.

"Alastair will be Rudolph the Reindeer who pulls Father Christmas's sleigh. He will have beautiful big antlers."

Michael grinned and nudged Alastair.

"Michael," smiled Miss Mopper, "I would like you to be my Stage Manager. You are *so* sensible. I know I can rely on you."

Michael sighed. He did not try to be sensible, but somehow he always was. He didn't think being a Stage Manager sounded very exciting. He wanted a costume and make-up like Alastair and Lennox.

"What does the Stage Manager do, Miss?" he asked.

"You will have to take care of all the props, like the silver sleigh. You will have to play tapes of music and crash the cymbals in the scarey parts . . . and you will be in charge of the stage curtains."

Michael brightened up at once. The new stage curtains were made of red velvet. Mrs Wilson the Headteacher had gone on and on about how expensive they were and how the children must never touch them. Michael would be the first person in the school to turn the big handle and open the curtains.

"Please, Miss Mopper, tell us what happens in your play," cried Crystal Cummings. "Tell us the whole story. What is it called?"

"It is called, 'A Crust at Christmas'," said Miss Mopper proudly.

"Eh?" said Lennox, puzzled.

"'A Crust at Christmas'," repeated Miss Mopper. "Listen and I will tell you all why.

Crystal you must listen more carefully than anyone, because you will be the Storyteller and sit on the stage with a big red book as if you were telling the audience a story."

"Crystal is the best reader, isn't she, Miss?" cried Alastair who didn't like reading very much.

"Yes, Crystal is very good," smiled Miss Mopper.

"And very fat," said Darrill.

"Shut up, Darrill," hissed Crystal's friend Maria.

"Shut up yourself, Greek Yoghurt," said Darrill and slid quickly away across the floor as Maria turned towards him.

"BE QUIET EVERYONE!" shouted Miss Mopper. "Settle down and listen. It is Christmas Eve. In front of the stage is a tall Christmas tree. It is decorated with stars and presents, and it has an angel on the top. I will play Christmas carols on the piano, and then out from the red velvet curtains comes the Storyteller with her book. She sits down by the Christmas tree and tells us that far, far away in a cold white land, Father Christmas is getting ready for his long journey round the world. The snow is falling and the stars are shining in the dark winter sky. Then some of our best dancers will do a swirling snowstorm dance! Who would like to dance?"

Lots of hands shot up and Miss Mopper quickly wrote down their names.

"Good," she said. "Then the Stage Manager opens the curtains and we see Father Christmas, dressed all in red, telling his goblins what to do as they load his sleigh with the presents they have been making all year. Hands up who wants to be a goblin ... fine. Then Father Christmas feeds his reindeer ready for their long journey."

"What will he feed them on, Miss?" called Alastair.

"Oh, I don't know, carrots or grass I suppose."

Alastair was disappointed. He had hoped for something nice.

"Maria," said Miss Mopper. "You're strong. Will you be the other reindeer and help Alastair to pull the sleigh?"

"Yes Miss, as long as I don't have to say anything," said Maria.

"You can make sure Alastair goes the right way and doesn't fall off the stage," whispered Michael.

Miss Mopper went on with her story.

"Then Father Christmas tells us that this Christmas is a very special one. This Christmas, for the very first time, there won't be a hungry child anywhere in the whole wide world!"

"Hurray!" shouted her class. Miss Mopper gave a little leap and her red curls bounced and shone around her face.

"The goblins are loading up Father Christmas's sleigh with toys they have made, and food that kind people have given them."

"Father Christmas is a sort of Bob Geldof, isn't he Miss?" said Lennox.

"Yes Lennox, if you say so. Mmmmm . . . I think we'll have a dear little Christmas fairy to wave her wand over the sleigh. Then the curtains close and the Storyteller tells us that the silver sleigh flies across the dark night sky until it hovers over a big city. It lands on the roof of a tall building at midnight. The toys on the sleigh come to life because it is a magic hour. Now then . . . Who wants to be a Jack-in-the-box or Action-Man or Miss Piggy? Or a sweet little teddy bear? Nobody wants to be a sweet little teddy bear? Oh dear."

2

A New Part for Crystal

Suddenly Miss Mopper crouched down and twisted her face so that it looked like a turnip lantern. "A *big dark shadow* falls over them all!" she whispered. Alastair gave a little scream.

"Is it King Kong, Miss, like in the film?" whispered Lennox.

"No. It is something far, far worse. Something truly evil. It is huge and green with grasping claws and burning eyes, red as hot coals."

The class gasped.

"Its name is The Gremlin of Greed," said Miss Mopper. "It is a monster that wants to keep everything for itself and not share it. It doesn't want Father Christmas to feed the Hungry Children."

"What does Father Christmas do?" asked Maria.

"He should challenge the Gremlin to a duel and then belt him round the head with a sack of toys," cried Lennox.

"No," cried Alastair, "he should run over him with the sleigh and squash him flat and the reindeer should trample him with their hooves."

"Push him over the edge of the building so that he smashes into hundreds of little green pieces," cried Michael.

"You are all so bloodthirsty," said Crystal calmly. "Father Christmas should have a long talk with the Gremlin and teach him how to be kind."

"Rubbish, Crystal!" shouted Lennox. "Oh, go on, Miss, what happens?"

"Father Christmas is locked up in the Gremlin's castle where the Gremlin keeps his piles of money and delicious food and warm clothes all for himself. The Gremlin frightens the reindeer away. Then he roars,

'Once a year in this magic hour
Great kindness can destroy my power.
Locked up in my castle you will stay,
But if somebody gives away
Everything he has, even though he
    might die,
The spell will be broken and away
    you'll fly!' "

"And then what, Miss?" pestered Lennox.

9

"Well . . . errr . . . actually I don't know because you see I had to finish my marking and so I haven't got to the end of the story yet."

"Oh MISS!" groaned the class and Miss Mopper looked ashamed.

"Who will be the Gremlin of Greed?" asked Michael.

"Darrill, of course," shouted Maria. "He doesn't even need any make-up."

"Shut up, Kebab," sneered Darrill. "I'm not being a Gremlin. I'm not being anything. I don't want to be in a stupid play." His friends looked away. They did want to be in the play, but they didn't want to quarrel with Darrill.

"Oh, Darrill," said Miss Mopper, "Don't you want to be a toy footballer or Action-Man? This is going to be THE BEST PLAY EVER!"

"Well it won't. It'll be the worst," scowled Darrill. "And you can't have a black Father Christmas."

"Why not?" cried Lennox.

Darrill frowned at the floor while he tried to think of a reason.

Crystal put up her hand and asked nervously, "Miss Mopper, please may I be the Gremlin of Greed?"

"What? Oh, Crystal, I can't imagine you frightening anybody bigger than an ant," laughed Miss Mopper.

"I can, I can!" shouted Crystal jumping to her feet. "Just watch me."

Miss Mopper smiled patiently as Crystal began to prowl round the hall. Her shoulders were hunched and her hands bent like claws. She pulled her face into a horrible leer and crept towards Lennox who was making everyone laugh by pretending to be a sweet little teddy bear.

Crystal crouched behind Lennox for a moment growling. Lennox stopped being a teddy bear and looked puzzled.

Then Crystal sprang at him with flashing

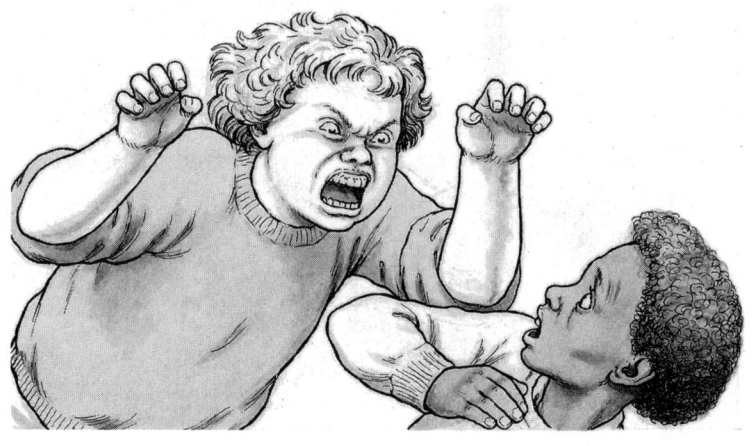

eyes and a blood-curdling scream. Lennox shrieked and threw himself to the floor.

Crystal stood up and smiled. Lennox peered through his fingers and laughed shakily.

"My goodness, Crystal, that was very good," cried Miss Mopper. "I didn't know you could act like that! Of course you must be the Gremlin. Will you be the Storyteller, then, John? Good. Oh, it's dinner-time already. Another rehearsal tomorrow, everybody. Off you go. QUIETLY."

"I wish we knew what happens in the end," said Crystal as they hurried out. "And what we are going to wear."

"We'll have make-up," cried Alastair. "And maybe my Mum will come to watch me."

"I'm sure she will," smiled Crystal. "And you'll have a big red nose."

"Last year Mr Jones's class did 'Cinderella'," said Michael. "Our play has to be even better than that. I hope nothing goes wrong."

"Why should it? Me as Father Christmas, and Crystal as the Gremlin of Greed?" said Lennox. "Never mind," he called to Darrill who was walking with his friends a little way behind. "You can be the Christmas Fairy."

3

No Sleigh for Santa

Things did go wrong with the Best Play Ever. They began to go wrong at the third rehearsal.

It was Friday. Mr Duckbody the Schoolkeeper was having a miserable morning. He dragged an enormous Christmas tree all the way back from the market. Then he spent an hour trying to get it through the front door. It was too tall standing up and too wide lying down. You couldn't see Mr Duckbody behind it. One of the Nursery children wandered out and burst into tears at the sight of a tree struggling to get into the school. The Nursery teacher scowled at Mr Duckbody as if it was all his fault.

Then Mr Duckbody had to go all the way back to the shop because he hadn't got a pot that was large enough for the tree. He came back and filled it with soil. As he stood up he saw two Nursery children hand-printing red painted hands all the way down his nice white corridor. He set off after them with a shout and had another argument with the Nursery teacher.

He came back to the pot to find Mugwump the school cat happily digging a hole. There was soil all over the floor.

When he came back from chasing Mugwump (who escaped onto the roof) Mr Duckbody filled the pot right up again and swept the
floor. Then he sighed.

Then he wandered into the hall and slumped
against the wall at the back. The ends of his
black moustache trailed down to his chin.

Miss Mopper cried, "This is where you
open the curtains, Michael. We will see Father
Christmas, the reindeer, the goblins and toys.
We will see the backcloth of snow and stars
that I painted last night." She yawned. "And
soon we will see a beautiful silver sleigh too."

Mr Duckbody gave a little cough. Everybody turned round.

"Pardon me, Miss Mopper," he said. "What
sleigh will that be?"

Miss Mopper's face turned red. "Ah, yes,
Mr Duckbody. I was going to ask you but I
kept forgetting . . . er, I've been so busy. Will
you make a sleigh for Father Christmas?
Please? You're so clever at making things."

Mr Duckbody sighed like the North Wind
and Lennox was sure that the stage curtains
moved.

"Miss Mopper, I am a Schoolkeeper. Some
call me a Janitor, some call me a Caretaker. I

15

am a busy man. I have libraries to lock, class-rooms to clean, vandals to chase and boilers to burn. I have to fight off cats and Nursery children so that I can plant a Christmas tree. I have not got a spare week to build you a sleigh." Mr Duckbody sounded as if he was talking to someone of three, not to Miss Mopper (who was very clever. She could read Russian, play the piano and she could windsurf.)

"Anyway, it would scrape the varnish off my stage," said Mr Duckbody.

"Oh no!" cried Miss Mopper. "We *must* have a sleigh. All right. If you don't want to help us with The Best Play Ever, Mr Duckbody, then I will make the sleigh myself. I spent until ten o'clock last night painting a backcloth of snow and stars. Tonight I will paint the Gremlin's castle. Next week I will make a sleigh as well. And I will make the runners out of cardboard so that there won't be a mark on your stage. All right, Mr Duckbody?" she cried. Her eyes were very bright and her voice sounded funny.

"Oh. All right then, Miss Mopper," said Mr Duckbody. He stood still for a moment. Then he wandered out of the hall and trod on a silver tree-decoration.

"We'll stay and help you make a sleigh, Miss," said Crystal. "Don't be upset."

"I am NOT UPSET, Crystal," shouted Miss Mopper, blinking hard. "Michael, pull that curtain back as far as it will go. Goblins, get on that stage this minute. Lennox. LENNOX! Say something."

Lennox jumped. He walked to the front of the stage and said,

"Hurry up goblins. Load the stuff.
Don't you get paid more than enough?
You've worked hours of overtime for
the girls and the boys
And made tea-sets and teddies and
wonderful toys.
You've hammered and painted all year
long.
You've made jigsaws, jack-in-the-
boxes and castles strong.
This year I'm wishing for even more.
I want the rich to help the poor.
I want to make the poor children and
babies happy
And give them warm clothes, good
food and . . . and . . . a nappy?"

Miss Mopper frowned. "You will have to think of something else for that last line, Lennox," she said.

There was a noise outside the hall door, a buzzing and chattering. The door burst open and Mr Jones stood there with his arms folded and his class trying to peep round him.

"My P.E. time, Miss Mopper," he said smugly.

"I didn't know you had P.E. now," said Miss Mopper. "And I'm sure you're early. Oh well. Back to the classroom everyone. And don't forget everything all over the weekend. Michael, may I have a word with you?"

That evening, Alastair wrote a letter to his mother. She did not live with Alastair and his father any more. The letter took him an hour.

Deer MUM
        I am a raindeer in the play
i am. ROODOLF THE RED KNOWS RAINDEAR
Maria is to   I am a Star Plees cum and woch me
Fryday nite You can sit wiv DAD
            luv
        ALASTAIR
                xXxXXXXxX

He drew holly leaves all round the page. They looked like crinkle-cut chips.

18

4

Chocolates for Everyone?

"Mum, Miss Mopper asked if Annie could be the Christmas Fairy," said Michael.

"Miss Mopper must be mad," said Michael's mother, washing up after Saturday lunch. "She doesn't know how awful your little sister can be."

"She does. I told her. She laughed. She said Annie will look sweet because she is only three and much smaller than the rest of us."

"She will look sweet, but she won't *be* sweet. Christmas Fairy, indeed. Ha!"

There was a ring at the door.

"I go!" shouted Annie and they heard her pounding down the hall.

Michael ran into the hall just in time to hear Annie screeching, "I want Big Bomber and a motor-bike and a BMX and a lorry and a machine gun and some chocolate mice and a new teddy bear because old teddy had an accident and chocolate money."

Michael gasped. Annie was talking to some-one in a long red coat and a hood trimmed with white fur.

"Who is it, dear?" called his mother from the kitchen.

"Father Christmas," he called back.

Father Christmas bent down and patted Annie on the head.

"Are you a good little girl, HO HO HO?" he said. "Do you help your Mum and Dad and big brother Michael? Do you deserve lots of lovely presents?"

"Yes!" shrieked Annie.

"No," said Michael.

Lennox laughed and pulled off the red hood. Annie stared.

"Why is Lennox in Father Christmas's dress?" she asked.

"My Dad borrowed the costume from work. I can wear it in the play. My Mum is going turn up the hem. I just *had* to come round and show you."

"It looks terrific," said Michael.

"Do you fancy a look around the shops?" asked Lennox.

"Good idea," said Michael.

"Can I come?" yelled Annie.

"NO," shouted Lennox and Michael to-gether. Annie pulled her 'I am going to cry' face but Michael's Mum said,

"You stay and help me put sequins on your pretty white dress, Annie. You're going to be a Christmas Fairy in Miss Mopper's play."

Annie clapped her hands. Lennox said, "What? A monkey with a wand?"

"I should leave that lovely red cloak here while you go out, love," said Mum to Lennox. "You'll get mud all over the hem."

Lennox had liked the idea of walking round dressed as Father Christmas, going HO HO HO and promising people Rolls-Royce cars and cherry cheesecake every day. But he knew Michael's Mum was right.

It was a cold December afternoon. Lennox and Michael hurried to the shops, their hands in their pockets to keep warm. They went into the department store. It was crammed full of families shopping for Christmas. It was so crowded that Lennox bounced off a big man's stomach and fell against a display of little snowmen with bowler hats. The snowmen flew in all directions like little white missiles.

"Oh, Maria, a snowman has flown into my bag," cried a voice they knew.

"Sorry, Crystal," called Lennox, picking up snowmen. "Some grown-ups are so RUDE. Well, fancy bumping into you two!"

"I'm bumping into everybody. It's so crowded. Let's go outside and walk round the shopping precinct. Then we can look in all the windows."

Each window was a box of delights. In the window of a bank, mean old Scrooge from 'A Christmas Carol' was counting his shining gold coins.

In another window there was a dappled rocking-horse as big as a Shetland pony, and a doll's house with twelve rooms and a family of dolls eating their Christmas dinner from a little table with candlesticks in the middle.

The best window of all was full of sweets. There were jars of pink and white sugared almonds like pearls and baskets full of marzipan fruits. There were hundreds of chocolates like little mountains, crowned with nuts and cherries. There were snowmen made of white chocolate. There were chocolate robins, chocolate goblins, chocolate bells and chocolate angels.

"I'll have that, and that, and THAT!" cried Lennox.

"Look at that Father Christmas with his sleigh full of rum truffles!" said Michael, licking his lips.

"I can't WAIT for Christmas," cried Maria. "And it's the play next week, I can't wait for that either!"

It was almost four o'clock. Darkness was filling the square. The lights on the tall Christmas tree glowed blue and deep red and the ropes of tinsel rustled and shone.

In the middle of the square stood the Salvation Army band. Their brass trumpets shone in the dark and the faces of the singers were bright. They began 'Silent Night'. The children listened and longed for Christmas.

"Do you think it will snow?" whispered Crystal, staring up at the cold clouds racing across the dark sky. She shivered.

"Maybe," said Michael. "I'm cold. Let's just look in one more window and go. Oh. This one's no good. There aren't any decorations, just some big photographs."

There were children in the photographs. One of them was about the same age as Annie, but Annie could have knocked him down with one shout. His arms and legs were as thin as matchsticks and his stomach looked blown-up and sore.

In another photograph, there were children old enough to be in Miss Mopper's class. They were lying down as if they had not got the strength to stand. There was no light in their sad eyes.

"They are the hungry children in the play," said Crystal. She thought to herself that Father Christmas would not be feeding them in real life.

The four children stared at the photographs and did not know what to say. Lennox remembered the window full of chocolates and felt sick.

"Father Christmas *could* help to feed them, you know," said Michael.

"What do you mean?" asked Maria.

"We could collect money for them when we do the play. This is a charity shop. They can give us the tins for the money and they can use it to buy food for the starving children."

"Great idea, Michael!" cried Lennox.

But the man in the charity shop said he couldn't give tins to children. He would only give them to a teacher.

"Our teacher will be in to see you next week!" announced Crystal. "She is called Miss Mopper. Of course she will let us collect the money! We would like five tins please. We have another friend called Alastair."

Maria was very quiet as they hurried home.

"Cheer up, Maria," said Crystal. "At least we can help those children a little bit."

"It's not just that," said Maria sadly. "I feel ill. I think I'll go to bed when I get home."

5

Volcanoes for Darrill

The classroom was strewn with streamers and stars and paper chains. Alastair was covered in glue and everything he touched stuck to him.

"We must practise the end of the play today," called Miss Mopper above the noise. "We only have a few days left. Oh dear! I MUST find time to make that sleigh."

"Miss Mopper, who breaks the Gremlin's spell?" pleaded Crystal.

"There is a knock on the castle door at a minute past midnight," said Miss Mopper. "It is a small boy in tattered clothes."

"I'm small!" cried Alastair eagerly as Lennox and Michael peeled paper off him.

"You are the Reindeer, Alastair. Jamie Brown is going to be the Poor Boy."

"Oh," said Alastair. He frowned at the paper star he had just cut out. It looked like a spider. He screwed it up and threw it into the bin.

"The Poor Boy wants to give away the only thing he has, a crust of bread. He is so kind that the Gremlin's power is destroyed and Father Christmas is set free."

"And the Gremlin of Greed falls on the floor in a rage and dies!" roared Crystal, clutching her throat. "AAAAGH!" she screamed, going cross-eyed.

"I'm worried about you, Crystal," frowned Miss Mopper. "You seem to have changed since I gave you this part. You're like Dr Jekyll and Mr Hyde. Anyway, at the end of the play, Father Christmas gives out food to the Hungry Children and we all sing 'Feed the World'. Come on, down to the hall before Mr Jones comes for his music lesson. There seem to be a lot of you absent today . . ."

When they reached the hall the stage curtains were closed.

"Just sit on the floor, everyone, while Michael opens the curtains," said Miss Mopper.

As the curtains swished open, the whole class gasped. Miss Mopper gasped too. On the stage was a beautiful silver sleigh. It had red wooden runners and a red seat. There were two decorated silver shafts at the front so that the reindeer could pull it. On one of the shafts someone had stuck a note.

"Read it, Michael!" cried Miss Mopper.

"It says, 'To Miss Mopper and her class, for The Best Play Ever. With love from Santa Duckbody'."

The hall door opened quietly and someone with a squeaky shoe crept in.

"Mr Duckbody, thank you! It's the most beautiful sleigh in the world!" said Miss Mopper.

Mr Duckbody twirled the ends of his moustache so that they curled right round his nose. "I had an hour to spare at the weekend," he said, "so I thought I might as well make a sleigh."

(Really he had worked on it all Saturday until two o'clock in the morning, and then painted it on Sunday afternoon.)

The hall doors burst open and in charged Mrs Wilson the Headteacher.

"What a wonderful sleigh, Mr Duckbody!" she called. "You are clever. Miss Mopper, I am afraid that I bring bad tidings. Mrs Nicolossi has just 'phoned. Maria has chickenpox. And Darrill's mother 'phoned. He has chickenpox too."

"It's a good job he didn't want a part after all, Miss," said Michael.

"Oh no," moaned Miss Mopper. "So that is why so many children are absent. Why does it have to be this week of all weeks? How can it be The Best Play Ever with half the cast away?" She hid her face in her hands.

"I hope we don't catch it," whispered Michael to Lennox. "We were with Maria on Saturday. We may have caught it from her. Or from anybody."

The whole class was worried sick.

All except Alastair. He was sorry that Maria had chickenpox. But now he would be the only Reindeer, and his mother would see him pull the sleigh all by himself.

Alastair was not at all sorry that Darrill had chickenpox. He hoped the spots were as big and red as volcanoes and that they itched all the time and left big scars on Darrill's face. He would have a lovely time at school without Darrill to bully him.

6

A Fright for the Fairy

Suddenly it was Friday night, time for costumes, make-up and excitement. Miss Mopper was rushing around fastening hooks and counting heads. Michael's mother was slapping on make-up and trying to keep Annie quiet.

"Listen!" called Miss Mopper. "I have Father Christmas, the Storyteller, the Gremlin and the Christmas Fairy. I have only got one Reindeer, three Snowflakes, two goblins and three toys. And I've only got four Hungry Children. Well, that will just have to do. Wait a minute . . . Where is Jamie Brown? Where is the Poor Boy?"

"He must have chickenpox, Miss," said Michael. "He wasn't well this morning. All Darrill's friends have got it."

"But I MUST HAVE A POOR BOY!" screeched Miss Mopper, pulling at her red curls. "I should never be doing a play on Friday the thirteenth."

"Can I be of any help?" asked Mr Duckbody, leaning in the doorway. Lennox sniggered at the thought of Mr Duckbody in short trousers, his moustache drooping forlornly as he held out his crust of bread.

"Only if you shrink, thank you, Mr Duckbody," sighed Miss Mopper. "Oh, you could collect money in Maria's tin at the end. If there is an end. 'A Crust at Christmas' indeed! More like 'Going Crackers at Christmas'."

"Somebody must play two parts," said Crystal, fixing a pair of sharp green horns on her head.

"Me, Miss Mopper, me me!" cried Alastair, pulling at the sleeve of her best white blouse.

"Alastair, stop wiping your red shiny nose on me!" snapped Miss Mopper, snatching her arm away.

"Please, Miss, I know what the Poor Boy says, and I'm small, and the Reindeer isn't in that scene, and – and – my Mum is in the audience, I know, I saw her arrive!"

Miss Mopper began to laugh hysterically. The class looked at each other. Was she going mad? Teachers did have nervous breakdowns.

"Why not, Alastair, why not?" she sighed. "Play both parts. Michael can give you the

Poor Boy's costume to put on backstage. Don't forget to wipe off Rudolph's red nose. The responsibility of two parts will be good for you!"

"She's mad," hissed Lennox. "Alastair can't play one part properly, certainly not two! Look after him, Michael."

"Right, everyone, it's time to go backstage," called Miss Mopper. "It's not our fault that our class has chickenpox. Just do your very best. Good Luck!"

The class waited. They could hardly breathe, they were so excited. The lights in the hall went out and the voices of the audience died away.

Miss Mopper was sitting by the piano at the front of the stage and every one else was behind. The Storyteller went out through the curtains and called out, as clear as a bell,

> "One Christmas Eve, in a land far away,
> Where polar bears and penguins play,
> Snow was falling, soft and white,
> Without a sound, in the dark night."

Michael played the tape of xylophone music for the Snowflakes' dance. It must have been good, because the audience clapped loudly and the three Snowflakes burst backstage flushed with pride.

"There's loads of people watching. It's pitch black out there. The Vicar and the Mayor and Mrs Pottle from the sweet shop are in the front row," whispered the Snowflakes.

Michael drew the curtains back with a great swish and the stage was flooded with light. The snowstorm backcloth and the shining sleigh looked splendid and the audience clapped again.

Father Christmas bowed. Then he spoke in a clear, ringing voice.

"Father Christmas is my name.

Or Santa Claus, it's one and the same.

My silver sleigh is pulled through the sky By Rudolph the Reindeer, who can sing, dance and fly!"

Father Christmas introduced the Reindeer to the audience with a wave of his red arm. And there, between the silver shafts of the sleigh stood Alastair, his head held high, crowned with the big antlers that Miss Mopper had made from wire and brown velvet. The spotlight shone straight down on him. The audience gasped. For not only did Rudolph have a big red shiny nose. He had big red spots all over his face as well.

Michael peeped down at Miss Mopper. She was in a panic. She mouthed, "GET HIM OFF" Michael shook his head. What could they do? Alastair must have been ill for a while, but he hadn't told anybody. He wasn't going to miss the play for anything. They were probably all infected now, and it was too late to do anything. Miss Mopper shrugged her shoulders and started to play 'Rudolph the Red-nosed Reindeer'.

Soon after they had finished the song, Michael had to send on the Christmas Fairy. "Annie, come on," he whispered. "Annie . . . oh no!"

Annie gazed up at him. She looked pretty in her white dress and silver wings. She had silver stars in her hair. But she had crumbs round her mouth, and the hand holding her wand was all covered in sticky brown chocolate.

"That food was for Father Christmas to give to the Hungry Children at the end," hissed Michael. There was nothing left. She had even eaten the crust of bread for the Poor Boy.

Michael quickly wiped Annie's face with a tissue and gave her a little push.

"Get on the stage," he hissed.

Annie smiled and waved her wand as she danced into the middle of the stage. The audience clapped. They thought she was lovely.

"Greedy little devil," muttered Michael to himself. What could he do? He must have some food for the Poor Boy and the Hungry Children! There might just be time before the next scene for him to get something from the school kitchen.

He let himself out of the little door at the back of the stage and ran along the outside of the hall, in at the front door, down the corridor to the white door marked KITCHEN.

It was pitch black. Michael felt all down the wall just inside the door but he could not find a light switch anywhere. He felt his way across the kitchen with his arms stretched out in front of him like a ghost.

Ah! This must be the fridge. He opened the door. There was only margarine and some milk inside. Of course, there would be new supplies on Monday.

He banged his leg as he felt the table. There were some large tin trays on the table. He

pulled off the lids which fell to the floor with a loud CLATTER.

Michael put his hand in the first tin. These must be apples, they were the right shape. They would do. He stuffed some up his jumper.

In another tin he found slices of something soft. It must be bread or sponge cake. Either would do. He grabbed as many pieces as he could carry or stuff in his pocket. He would explain to Cook on Monday what had happened.

Then he ran back along the corridor, out of the front door, along the outside of the hall and in at the little door at the back of the stage. Just in time!

Gasping for breath, Michael saw Annie standing by the sleigh. The audience was listening to Lennox. Annie was bored. She had forgotten that there was an audience at all. She took off her shoes.

Father Christmas cried,
"So we fly, far out of sight,
On our great journey through the night."
And Annie took her dress off.
Michael closed the curtains as fast as he

could, grabbed Annie and stuffed her back into her clothes.

"Christmas Fairies do not strip!" he hissed, and pushed her back on the stage. Then he opened the curtain again for the scene on the rooftop.

Everything went all right. Then the Gremlin of Greed appeared and the audience jumped in their seats. Crystal roared,

> "I am the Gremlin of Greed! And I shall not share.
> My wealth with ANYONE. I DON'T CARE!"

The Gremlin's eyes flashed like red coals in her green face. She had long red spiky nails like claws and she cackled wickedly at the little Christmas Fairy.

"Help! Mum! Mike! Help!" screamed Annie and fled off the stage and into Michael's arms. The audience thought this was very exciting (except for Annie's Mum). Father Christmas's shoulders were shaking too, but Michael knew this was with laughter, not fright.

Crystal was acting as if she was in a horror film. She prowled across the stage and roared at Alastair,

"Rudolph, Begone! Your nose so bright
Will NOT light Santa's way tonight!"

Rudolph trotted off the stage. He pulled off his brown velvet reindeer costume with the little black hooves, and put on the tattered trousers that Michael gave him. Michael closed the curtains and let down the backcloth for the scene in the Gremlin's castle. He opened them again and the play went on.

"Here's the crust of bread," said Michael, pulling a piece of something from his pocket.

"Ugh! It's all soggy," said Alastair. He rubbed off his red nose with a tissue. Then he grinned. "Here I go, Michael. I'm the Poor Boy now!" He was spottier than ever.

"WAIT, Alastair!" cried Michael.

It was too late. The Poor Boy trotted across the stage and knocked three times on the big painted door to the Gremlin's castle.

And there he waited in the spotlight. The Poor Boy. With his tattered trousers, his spots, and his antlers.

7

Pudding for Mr Duckbody

Father Christmas did not have much to say at the beginning of the next scene. This was lucky, because he could not stop giggling. The poor Gremlin felt as if her face would crack in half as she looked at the Poor Boy in antlers (or the Reindeer in trousers).

Head held high and antlers wobbling, Alastair made his speech.

> "If I were a rich boy, I would give my
>   money.
> But I'm a very Poor Boy. That's not
>   funny!
> Look everybody, here's my little soggy
>   crust.
> In the power of Kindness I will trust.
> Horrible old Gremlin! I will destroy
> Your power by being a kind Poor
>   Boy!"

Something dripped off the crust as Alastair held it high. He cried,

"I hope my little bit of bread
  Will make the Gremlin drop down
  dead!"

The Gremlin threw herself to the floor,
screaming and thrashing and Michael crashed
the cymbals together until she lay still. The
audience cheered to see her wicked power destroyed and Annie shouted, "Kill it. Horrible
Gremlin! Good, it's dead!"

The play was almost over. Father Christmas
snatched the food from Michael at the side of
the stage to feed the Hungry Children.

Michael did not want to watch him give out
the food. The Poor Boy's crust had been bad
enough.

The Hungry Children cried, "Ugh," as Father Christmas gave out the raw onions and cold Yorkshire Pudding dripping with greasy gravy which Michael had thought were apples and bread. Someone said, "I'm not THAT hungry, Lennox!"

Father Christmas shouted,

> "You'll be glad to know, all you Dads and Mums,
> That the children had big fat full-up tums."

"Sing up. SING UP!" cried Miss Mopper, hoping that the audience would not hear the Hungry Children moaning about their food. The class sang, 'Do they know it's Christmas?' and the audience joined in. The Hungry Children slid their greasy Yorkshire Pudding out of sight under the red velvet curtains as they swished together. Then they sang loudly too.

After everyone had sung 'Feed the World' the play was finished. The audience cheered and clapped and stamped their feet. Miss Mopper was slumped over the piano.

Mrs Wilson the Headteacher clambered up onto the stage. She was wearing a smart green glittery dress and she had been to the hairdressers.

"Mothers and Fathers. Friends. Brothers and Sisters, Mr Mayor, Reverend Crayfish. Mrs Pottle. Everybody! I am sure you will all agree that 'A Crust for Christmas' was very, very good. In fact, I will go so far as to say that it was The Best Play Ever!"

The class cheered and the audience clapped again. Then there was a long wait while a little boy from the Infants heaved himself up onto the stage carrying a big bunch of flowers. Then he climbed down again. At last he saw Miss Mopper by the piano, and gave her the flowers.

Everyone cheered. Then Mrs Wilson said, "Some of Miss Mopper's class are collecting money for children who are really starving. Please, everyone, give as much as you can."

(And everybody did. They collected over one hundred pounds. The man in the charity shop was amazed.)

"Mike," whispered Lennox, as they stood at the back of the hall rattling their tins, "there's Alastair's Mum!"

"She looks really pleased with him," Michael whispered back. "He did very well, especially when you remember that he's Alastair."

"Do you think his Mum will come back to live with them now that he's done something well?" asked Lennox.

"Shut up, you two!" hissed Crystal, her red eyes flashing in her green face.

But it was too late. Alastair had heard them. He turned round.

"No, she can go back to her new home now," he said brightly. "I only wanted her to come and see me in the play. I wanted her to see me be a star. That's all."

And Alastair smiled at his mother.

"Hmmph! I bet we get chickenpox just in time for Christmas," grumbled Lennox. But they didn't.

"Miss Mopper, the play was wonderful!" said Mr Duckbody. "I even had to wipe away a tear."

"I wonder if his tears were from crying or laughing," whispered Crystal.

"I wonder if he'll laugh or cry when he finds out that his beautiful polished stage is all covered with Yorkshire Pudding and greasy gravy," said Lennox.

But by the time Mr Duckbody cleaned his stage, he was so full of the Christmas spirit that he didn't even notice.